1~99

WHIT

Koko Brown

WHITE

OBERON BOOKS
LONDON

WWW.OBERONBOOKS.COM

First published in 2017 by Oberon Books Ltd
521 Caledonian Road, London N7 9RH
Tel: +44 (0) 20 7607 3637 / Fax: +44 (0) 20 7607 3629
e-mail: info@oberonbooks.com
www.oberonbooks.com

A catalogue record for this book is available from the British
Library.

PB ISBN: 9781786823847
E ISBN: 9781786823854

Cover edit and design: Chris Lincé
Cover photography: Jameela Elfaki

Printed and bound by 4EDGE Limited, Hockley, Essex, UK.
eBook conversion by CPI Group (UK) Ltd, Croydon, CR0 4YY.

This play is for anyone who has ever felt like *the other*.

An early version of the play was first performed at the Roundhouse, London, on 4th June 2017. The completed version was performed at Ovalhouse Theatre, London, on 15th November 2017.

The character is gender and age non-specific.

This play incorporates music throughout. The performer is encouraged to create music live in any format or style that suits them, and to find their own rhythm within the poetry.

There is pre-show music playing while the audience enter. The song choice should represent what the performer listened to when they were younger.

This text went to press before the end of rehearsal and may differ slightly from the show as performed.

TRACKLIST

Underscore #1

Half Of You

Privilege

War With Yourself

Underscore #2

The Valley

Other Side

Roots

INHALING

The stage is set with LOOP STATION #1 upstage left, LOOP STATION #2 downstage right, two MICROPHONES on stands and a CASSETTE PLAYER downstage left with various TAPES scattered around it.

She enters and smiles warmly at the audience. There is no fourth wall. She walks over to the CASSETTE PLAYER, picks it up and presses play. Michael Jackson's 'Black Or White' plays from rap to end of chorus.

She stops the tape.

That's it. That's the show. Thanks for coming.

    Beat.

Just kidding. So, I wanted to make a show about race. Specifically about being mixed race. And I wanted to share the stories of all other mixed-race people. I wanted to share their experiences and what it's like being mixed race. I even had an event where I got some mixed-race people in a room and we all just spoke about what it was like being mixed race.

Then I realised that it's unfair to say that I can tell the story of all mixed-race people, because I can't. So instead I decided to focus on the one mixed-race person that I know the best. *(Aside.)* It's me. The show that I was going to make, it started a little bit like this –

    She cues UNDERSCORE #1 from LOOP STATION #1 and is suddenly in a spotlight. She layers a simple melody. The music is reflective with a steady beat.

I always knew what I was.
I was female. I was mixed race. Aged one.
One of two people of colour, me and my brother,
on my mother's side
Basically being brown in, on and around my mother's white, Irish side
Never really knowing the other side.

I always knew what I was.
I was female, mixed race, aged three
With a doll who kind of looked like me
Suddenly it wasn't two, it was three
Brown babies in the family.

I always knew what I was.
I was female, mixed race, aged five
With hair so alive,
Tactically taunting my mum
Tresses refusing to be calm

I always knew what I was.
I was female, mixed race, aged eight.
'Girl Power' growled through timid teeth!
I was never really a beast.
I was actually quite quiet and shy
So I wondered why I always had to be Scary Spice.
Now I know why.

I always knew what I was.
I was female, mixed race, aged eleven.
Wanted to try make-up
Mum said yeah, so I got made up
Tried her lipstick,
Her eyeliner
Her eyeshadow.
But how was I to know
That her 'nude' foundation wouldn't go
With my inherited, nude skin tone

I always knew what I was.
I was female, mixed race, aged thirteen.
Listened to 'white music'.
Like Fall Out Boy, Panic, Paramore
I practically perfected the angsty-teenager-emo-eyeliner look.

I always knew what I was.
I was female, mixed race, aged fifteen.
I cut my uncontrollably curly hair into a front fringe
Yes, it did look as bad as you're imagining.

I always knew what I was.
I was female, mixed race, aged seventeen.
The fringe grew out. Jeans filled out.
(Motions to chest.) Not everything filled out
But you can't win 'em all!

I always knew what I was.
I was female, mixed race, aged nineteen
Realised that I liked boys the same way I liked my music…
White.

I always knew what I was.
I was female, mixed race, aged twenty-one.
Tired of looking like Tamika or Keisha or Elisha from endz
Wanting to be distanced from that,
Wanting to be cut off
I cut it off.
Some people mourned the loss of my trademarked curls
Whereas I celebrated the short back and sides.

I always knew what I was.
I was female, mixed race, aged twenty-two

    Into mic.

'Who's your friend over there?
The black girl with the short hair.'

    She stops the music.

Where?
Me?
Nah, can't be.
You see I think you'll find I'm mixed.
I'm as much black as I am white.

INHALING

SPIRALLING

Someone once said, 'To be a mix of races is to be raceless, and yet that had never been my reality.'

In reality I could never be that. I thought I knew what I was but…

To be a mix of races is to belong to two worlds.

You have the best of both worlds.

But you still have to pick a world.

You have to pick a side.

To audience.

Pick a side. Pick a side. Pick a side. Pick a side. Pick a side. Pick a side. Pick. A. Side.

But make sure it's the side they picked for you.

Where do you stand?

What do you choose?

Where do you fit – it doesn't matter where you fit because the one-drop rule decided it for you.

It has been decided for you.

And yes that is what I am but it is not just what I am.

And I am at war.

And I am torn between what I knew and what I know.

What I know…

The following list can be edited so that it is true for the performer.

I know that I am female.
I know that I am twenty-four.
I know that I am five foot eight.
I know that I have never had a nosebleed.
I know that I have four brothers and one sister.
I know that my mum is Irish.
I know that my dad is Jamaican.

I know that this has to be about me.
I know that it can't be general.
I know that it has to be about how I always knew what I was.
I was female, mixed race, aged twenty-two

Into mic.

'Who's your friend over there?
The black girl, with the short hair.'

Where?
Me?
Nah, can't be, because I'm mixed.
I'm as much black as I am white. Duh!

INHALING

SPIRALLING

LANDING

She cues the pre-recorded opening of HALF OF YOU from LOOP STATION #2. The music is bouncy and playful.

    You.   *(Recorded in layered harmonies.)*

    Half of you,
    I'm so proud to be half of you

I am half my mum.
Half of her has made me me and half of her is me.
I've got half of her short temper and half of her love of reality TV.
Half of her knowledge of how to fix a washing machine without any electrical qualifications (or actual knowledge of how to fix a washing machine).
Half of her knowing how to handle heartbreak well and half of her not knowing how to handle heartbreak well.
Half of her mental illnesses.
Half of her ability to preserve.
Half of her ease with children.
Well, just about half of her ease with children.
She is really good with children, she's like the child-whisperer or something!
Half of her love of White Musk and pretty much anything else the Body Shop dishes out.
Half of the wooden spoon catching the back of my leg when I talked back. Yeah, I got that from her.
A lot of love. Yeah, I get that from her.

    (Sings.)
    Half of you, half of you
    I'm so proud to have a part of you

The tone or melody should change for the following chorus.

    You, half of you,
    I'm so proud to be half of you

I am half my dad.
Half of him has made me me and half of him is me.
I've got half of his big smile and the laugh lines that go with it.
Our faces are built the same.
We are identical by features and identical by last name.
I've got half of his characteristic curls,
Half of his time-keeping skills,
Half of his golfing skills,
Half of his relaxed attitude,
Half of his ability to hold a grudge.
Half of his love of museums, of his love of art, of his love of
culture, of his love of nature.
Love is in his nature.
Half of the first man I have ever loved and half of the first man
who has ever left and half of the first man I have ever hated.
Half of what I look for in the men I've dated and half of
what I should avoid in the men I've dated.
I've got a whole bunch of daddy issues…but that's another show.
A lot of love. Yeah, I get that from him.

> *(Sings.)*
> Half of you, half of you
> I'm so proud to have a part of you

She fades the music out.

INHALING

SPIRALLING

LANDING

EXPLORING

And I'm aware that those two halves come with some privilege.

She cues the pre-recorded opening of PRIVILEGE from LOOP STATION #1. The mood changes from naturalistic to a more stylised tone. The music is upbeat, playful with knowing or mischievous undertones. Throughout the song musical layers are added to create a sickly sweet, cheesy backing track.

> I've got a lot of privilege
> But I'm not white
> So I, can't call it white privilege
> I've got a lot of privilege
> But I'm half white
> So what should I call this half-white privilege?
> Is 'mixed' privilege a thing?
> Should I call it 'mixed-race privilege', is that even
> a thing?
>
> I had that good hair
> Had those nice 3C curls
> Then I cut it all off
> Did I lose privilege as well?

Is that how is works? I don't really know –

> Is 'good-hair privilege' a thing?
> Should I call it '3C privilege,' is that even a thing?
>
> Got the best of both worlds
> Full 'black' lips and a thin, 'white' nose.
> They say: 'You think you're better 'cause you're
> lightskinned, but we came in the same boat.
> Hashtag Team Lightskin, bet you were one of those.'

No, I wasn't actually.

> Is 'lighty privilege' a thing?
> I don't deal with colourism so I guess that it's a thing.

I still cast as a black girl
The one-drop rule makes sure of that
Doesn't stop me getting roles though
Just the right amount of black

I'm black enough to tick a box but not too black. Handy right?

Is 'one-drop privilege' a thing?
When they cast Zoe as Miss Simone it totally was
a thing!

Then there's always that one guy
That feels that it's alright
To ask dumb questions cause I'm half black and
half white,
They always ask me something like…

'What if a white child with cancer only had three weeks
left to live and their dying wish to the Make A Wish
Foundation was to be able to say the N word just once.
Are you telling me it's not okay for a white person to say
the N word in that instance?'

*She stops the music and shares a moment with the audience.
After a beat she brings PRIVILEGE back in.*

Is half-nigger privilege a thing?
They feel like they can ask those questions so I guess
that it's a thing.
Not exactly a 'privilege' but it definitely is
something.

I can't be cross, I can't be mad
'Cause I've got skin lighter than a paper bag
I would've been allowed to read
And I would have been allowed to be in the master's
house

Probably would have been called a half-breed or a mongrel,
but at least I wasn't working in the hot sun all day right?

Is brown-bag privilege a thing?
I'm pretty sure, I heard before, it used to be a thing

Got a lot of privilege
And I'm half white
I've got the best of both worlds baby

Got a lot of privilege
And I'm half black
I've got the best of both worlds baby

Got a lot of privilege
And I'm half white, I'm half black
I've got the best of both worlds baby

I've got the best of both worlds baby
I've got the best of both worlds baby
I've got the best of both worlds baby
I've got the best of both worlds…
(She trails off, allowing the music to fade with her.)

INHALING

SPIRALLING

LANDING

EXPLORING

CONFRONTING

I always knew what I was. I was female, mixed race, aged twenty-two.

Into mic.

'Who's your friend over there?
The black girl, with the short hair.'

Where?
Me?
Nah, can't be.
You see, I think you'll find I'm mixed.
I'm as much black as I am white.
Isn't it obvious?!

She hits the MIC to her chest to create a steady drum beat. She records this into LOOP STATION #2 as the base rhythm for WAR WITH YOURSELF.

You don't know who you are
You, you're being torn apart from the inside out
You don't know where you fit
You want to escape it but can't figure a way out

Hey kid get your gun, get your gun, get your gun,
Hey kid get your gun, get your gun.
You are in a war, in a war, in a war,
You are in a war with yourself.

Two worlds collided
And here you are
When worlds collide
Where do you stand?

Who do you choose?   *(Recorded into loop station.)*
Where do you stand?   *(Recorded over previous line.)*

Hey kid get your gun, get your gun, get your gun,
Hey kid get your gun, get your gun.
You are in a war, in a war, in a war,
You are in a war with yourself.

Hey kid get your gun, get your gun, get your gun,
Hey kid get your gun, get your gun.
You are in a war, in a war, in a war,

She stops the music abruptly.

You are in a war with yourself.

INHALING

SPIRALLING

LANDING

EXPLORING

CONFRONTING

SUBMERGING

I always knew what I was.
I was female, mixed race, aged twenty-three.
In New York City.
And there's Broadway and the Empire State and there
are people.
So many people.
And there's police and more people and police and people
and a banner.
What does it say?

                I get caught up   I get swept away–
'Are you okay?'

                        Asks some unknown face.
And police and people and police and people and sirens
and a banner.
What does it say?
(Into mic.) 'Hashtag Black Lives Matter.'
And suddenly, everything is black.

    *Images and video clips representing her version of black culture
    are projected onto her.*

And my culture is black.
     And my people are black.
And my people are succeeding,
     And my people are winning,
         And my people are dominating,
And that culture is now my culture.
And my culture is music
         and dance
            and cakewalk
               and crip walk
                  and carnival.
And my culture matters
            and black lives matter.
And my culture full
       and dense
         and rich.

And my culture is being appreciated.
And my culture is being appropriated
        and forcibly integrated.
And my culture adoring the melanin skin it's in.
It's appreciating that good hair.
That 4c-hair,
   kinky,
     curly,
       can't-quite-calm-it-today hair,
    cornrows,
      weave in,
        Marley twist,
          natural hair.
And I am a descendant of
      Kings
       and
        Queens.
And I am a descendant of
      servants
       and
        slaves.

And a descendant of my father.
       And my grandfather.
And I am what they are.
And I stand for what they stood for and so much more.

*The following pieces of text are randomly recorded, overlapping
each other, creating a cacophony of sound which underscores itself.
This plays live to the audience.*

And I am not ghetto.

And I am not a lighty.

And I don't speak white
because I speak politely.

And I, too, have a dream.

And I, too, know why
the caged bird sings.

And I don't know why
they won't stop shooting.

And Michael Brown,
'Hands up, don't shoot.'

And black power.

And 'I can't breathe'.

And Damilola Taylor

And Sandra Bland

And Stephen Lawrence

Tamir Rice, male, black,
aged twelve

And black lives matter.

And black lives matter.

And black lives matter.

*(Fragments heard in the
background.)*

Not ghetto–

Not ghetto–A lighty–

Not ghetto–A lighty–
      Speak whit–Politely–

Not ghetto–A lighty–
      Speak whit–Politely–
         Drea–

She walks to LOOP STATION #2 and creates UNDERSCORE #2. It is fast-paced, internal and heavy with low notes. Both pieces play over one another.

She watches the projection as the images get faster and faster. It stops on a screen which reads: 'To be a mix of races is to be raceless [...] and yet that had never been my reality.' – Varaidzo.

INHALING

SPIRALLING

LANDING

EXPLORING

CONFRONTING

SUBMERGING

DROWNING

She stops the recorded text on LOOP STATION #1 and stands in a harsh white spotlight. UNDERSCORE #2 continues to play.

I always knew what I was.
I was female, black, aged one.
One of two people of colour, me and my brother,
on my mother's side.
Basically being brown in, on and all around my mother's
white, Irish side.
Never really knowing the other side.

I was female, black, aged three.
The only black kid with with a white mum in my nursery.

I was female, black, aged five.
Hadn't seen my dad for two years.
I was cut off from that life.
No longer had ties to the other side

I was female, black, aged eight
I was actually quite quiet and shy and I never spoke up to
say that I didn't want to be Scary Spice.
But what can you say when you're the only person of
colour in an all-white space?

I was female, black, aged eleven.
Wanted to try make-up, mum said yeah so I got made up.
But being brought down by constant micro-aggressions
takes a toll.
'Well honey, when God was making black people he told
them to get into the Stop And Search position with their
hands against the wall and that's why your palms are
white!'

I was female, black, aged thirteen.
You don't know who Kano is?
You don't don't listen to Boy Better Know?
You don't watch Channel U?
Then what do you listen to?

Emo?
Oh…

I was female, black, aged fifteen.
Wanting to fit in, just wanting to be seen,
I cut my uncontrollably curly hair into a front fringe.

I was female, black, aged seventeen.
Sitting in my grandma's living room,
Looking to my dad for help,
Hoping he is understanding that I'm not understanding
my grandmother's native patois.
Her mother tongue isn't native to me.

I was female, black, aged nineteen.
I realised that I liked boys the same way I liked my
music… White.
'No, I don't date black boys.'
And yes, I'd love a spoonful of Internalised Anti-Blackness
in my cup of Preference thanks!

I was female, black, aged twenty.
Tired of looking like Tamika or Keisha or Elisha from endz –

She abruptly stops UNDERSCORE #2.

What's wrong with looking like Tamika or Keisha or Elisha
from endz?

Pause.

WADING

DROWNING

I always knew what I was. I was female…aged twenty-two.

Into mic.

'Who's your friend over there?
The black girl, with the short hair.'

Where?
Me?
Nah, can't be because I'm mixed.
I'm as much white as I am black!

I wish I could take that back.

She creates the opening loop to THE VALLEY – this is slow-paced but steady with slightly haunting undertones.

Walk through the valley of the ones you love
Push through the water it is made of blood

She creates distance between herself and the audience. This is an internal conflict which is only made external to help her find answers.

A lot of my journey was questioning
Questioning who I was and why and how I identify.
Why being mixed race made me so proud.
Why being labelled as 'black' was such a bad thing.
Why I wore my anti-blackness like a badge of honour.
My narrative has always been anti-black.
Looking back I wonder if my dad has something to do with that?
Is the absence of dad equal to the absence of black?
I wonder if being drowned in whiteness,
Gasping for the smallest piece of black culture,
Grasping at the smallest pieces of that culture,
Just to feel like I belonged to that culture,
Always feeling rejected by that culture,
Was that the base of my 'preference'?

Somehow proud to say that I'd never date a black boy for
no reason other than the fact he was a black boy.
Preference can become a fetish when you're the oppressor.
But what about when you use that preference to suppress?
What then?
Does my lack of knowledge for that culture allow me to
oppress that culture?
And how did I have the audacity to say it
      out loud,
           to
         s p r e a d
                  i t
                        a r o u n d ?

Infecting the atmosphere where I stood so proud.
I move forward knowing that I have changed.
                        Though I still carry shame.

*She records a simple melody, as if she's coaxing an answer from
thin air, then layers another, somewhat pained, melody on top.*

    Walk through the valley of the ones you love
    Push through the water it is made of blood

Our narrative has always been anti-black.
It is absorbed through the pores and so it p
                o
                  u
                r
                   s
                      i
                        n,

drowning your next of kin in the pool of social media
hashtags, of skin lightening.
Photoshopping the way we see beauty.

Looking through their bifocal lense,
                          short-sighted,
                                    close-minded.
                                    Obviously,
this is not the way that things should be but then why,
                                    why,
did I feel the need to hide from the sun?
Staying in the shade is no fun.
Saying, 'I don't wanna get a tan', 'I don't wanna get too dark.'
Then what does that mean for my naturally dark-skinned
friends?
Does that mean I subconsciously shed shame on them?
Even though their beauty b
                    r
                        e
                            a
                                k
                                    s
                            down
                                every beauty standard set.
They set milestones and surpass them in one fell swoop.
They
        b
      r
        e
          a
            k
                    down barriers that were built to break them.
So what does it mean for those friends, when I protest to
letting in the Vitamin D because I believed that getting
dark wasn't for me?
I look back at that version of myself ashamed. I move
forward knowing that I have changed.

(Sings.)

Walk through the valley of the ones you love
Push through the water it is made of blood

The water is not too deep
You will not drown
As long as you chose to keep
Your head above the ground

Walk through the valley of the ones you love
Push through the water it is made of blood

She silences the opening loop, leaving just the melody.

Walk through the valley of the ones you love

She allows the melody to play once more before silencing it.

EMERGING

WADING

DROWNING

The first time I'd ever felt black was when I joined a Black
Lives Matter march, accidentally.
I stumbled and fell into the black community and suddenly
it felt like Hashtag Black Girl Magic applied to me.
                                        But does it apply to me?
Or am I still too white for the black community?
Will I always be too black for the white community?
Can I find a way for them to both fit inside of me?
Where do they fit inside of me?

> *She records vocal percussion as the opening loop of OTHER SIDE.*
> *This is fast-paced and frustrated.*

All I'll ever be, is on the other side,
I'll forever be on the other side.

I stumbled over my words
Lists of things I shouldn't say
I tumbled over my thoughts
Wished I wasn't made this way.
Why was I made this way?

All I'll ever be, is on the other side,
I'll forever be on the other side.

> *A line of text is projected. The house lights come up a little and*
> *she addresses the audience directly.*

You are looking at words that people have actually said to me.
I'd like you to say them to me.

> *She enters the audience and secretly records them saying each*
> *phrase as it appears.*

Black people don't listen to Fall Out Boy.

How mixed race are you?

I wanna have mixed-race babies so they look like you.

People like you are occupying the space of black people.

If you had to pick a side, which would you pick?

You're half black, you must be able to twerk.

You don't know who Skepta is, aren't you half black?

But where are you really from?

Halfbreed.

Black people don't listen to Panic! At The Disco.

If all the black people were rounded up and put on a boat,
you'd be with them. You're no different.

What do you mean you don't understand patois?

The more mixed race people there are in the world,
the less racism there will be.

You're not really black though.

You're not really white though.

You're such a bounty bar.

You're a bit of an ethnic mongrel aren't you.

Wow, you're so exotic!

Half-caste kid.

Where are you from?

Your hair is so nice. You're so lucky you're mixed!

On paper you're black.

For a mixed person, you're acting very white.

You think you're nice just because you're mixed.

Once she's at the end of the projection, she returns to her LOOP STATION.

Each of the following verses is recorded.

> What are you?
> What are you?
> What are you?
> Woah.

The following verse is repeated while building in harmony and tone, representing individual people.

> What are you?
> What are you?
> What are you?
> Woah.

She sings the following verse over what has been recorded. This should be slightly out of rhythm with everything else. It should be exhausting to listen to. It's being drilled into her mind and is repeated as many times as necessary.

> All I'll ever be
> All I'll ever be
> All I'll ever be

She instantly removes everything but the 'What are you?' section. She lets it play through once, listening to the voices questioning her identity. Then simultaneously stops that section and plays the audience track.

Black people don't / were put on a boat / listen to Fall Out
/ you're no different / how mixed race are you / babies
so they look like you / people like you are occupying /
half-caste kid / the space of black people / had to pick a
side, which would you / half black, you must be able to
twerk / rounded up / don't know who Skepta is, aren't you
/ people like you / half black / but where are you really /
halfbreed / black people don't listen to / who Skepta is /
black people don't listen to / like you are occupying / half
breed / space of black people / if all the black people /
no differ / boat, you'd be with them / paper you're black
/ no different / like you are occupying the space of black
people / what do you mean you don't understand / more
mixed race people there are / patios / the less racism there
will be / not really black / you're not really white / you are
occupying the space of / bounty bar / listen to Panic! At
The Disco / you are occupying the space of black people
/ to Panic! At The / bit of an ethnic mongrel aren't / so
exotic / half-caste kid / where are you fro / hair is so /
black people don't / lucky you're mix / paper you're black
/ mixed person, you're acting very / the black people /
halfbreed / rounded up and put on a boat, you'd be with
/ you must be able to / mixed race babies / no different /
put on a boat / so they look li– / aren't you w– / really fr– /
rounded u– / very whi– / people don– / Skep– / bree– /
with th– / aren–

> *She listens to the audience track and starts repeating some of the
> lines to herself. She then starts mimicking the way they are said
> and repeating lines sarcastically. She continues until this becomes
> overwhelming and she pulls the lead from her LOOP STATION
> cutting off all sound instantly. For a second a slight electrical
> buzz is heard in the background.*

EXHALING

EMERGING

WADING

DROWNING

I wanted to say something. Something with meaning but I don't have the words.

> *Pause.*

I'm sorry.

> *She breathes. Walks over to the CASSETTE PLAYER, sits down and stares at the tapes.*

I don't have the words. I thought I'd be able to but I can't.

> *Beat.*

I have these tapes. This is me.

> *She picks a tape up, puts it in the CASSETTE PLAYER and listens.*

> *The following songs can be edited so that they are true for the performer. These should relate to the audience entrance music from the beginning.*

> *She picks one up, puts it in the cassette player and listens. Whitney Houston's 'It's Not Right But It's Okay' plays.*

> *She searches through the tapes, chooses one and plays it. Busted's 'Crashed The Wedding' plays.*

> *She searches through the tapes, chooses one and plays it. Aqua's 'Barbie Girl' plays.*

> *She searches through the tapes, chooses another and plays it. Shanks & Bigfoot's 'Sweet Like Chocolate Boy' plays.*

> *She gets up with the CASSETTE PLAYER and goes to LOOP STATION #1. She stops the CASSETTE PLAYER.*

> *Beat.*

She begins to sing a cappella.

> Oh my roots
> They are buried in the ground
> They help me to grow
> And they hold me down.

She records this and repeats it a few times, adding harmonies, creating a chorus of herself. She then adds a simple supporting melody. The music continues to play in the background.

She re-plugs in the LOOP STATION and tidies the cassette tapes, bringing herself and her surroundings back to neutral.

I always knew what I was.

BLACKOUT.

ABOUT THE AUTHOR

Born and bred in North West London and 'works well with others', according to all of her school reports. Koko is a theatre-maker & spoken word artist, who uses her loop station as an additional limb. She takes pride in her roots and creates work about being the 'other', mainly focusing on race, mental health, gender, and identity.
She is currently an Associate Artist at Ovalhouse theatre and an Alumni Resident Artist at the Roundhouse.

Visit her website for more information about the show and to download the soundtrack:

heykoko.com   **@TheKokoBrown**